HANG GLIDING
AND
PARASAILING

By Toni Will-Harris

PUBLISHED BY
Capstone Press
Mankato, Minnesota USA

CIP
LIBRARY OF CONGRESS CATALOGING IN
PUBLICATION DATA

Will-Harris, Toni.
    Hang gliding and parasailing / Toni Will-Harris.
        p. cm. — (Action sports)

ISBN 1-56065-058-3:
1. Hang gliding—Juvenile literature. 2. Parakiting—Juvenile
literature. 3. Hang gliding—History—Juvenile literature.
      I. Title. II. Series.
      GV764.W52   1989
      797.5'5—dc20   89-38672
                                            CIP
                                            AC

PHOTO CREDITS

Stephen Datnoff: 4, 7, 12, 16, 17, 23, 24, 25, 27, 28, 39, 42, 47

Jay Carroll: 8, 14,19, 31, 40

Sport Chutes Over Texas, Inc.: 32, 34, 35, 37

Capstone Press
P.O. Box 669, Mankato, MN, U.S.A. 56002-0669

CONTENT

SOARING WITH THE BIRDS

The sun rises. A light breeze blows. You stand a few feet from the edge of a cliff. The plastic skin of your red hang glider shivers in the breeze.

You attach your harness to the hang glider and begin to run forward. The wing of the glider floats above you. The edge of the cliff gets closer. As you take the last step, you feel the wind catch the sail and you sail into the sky.

As you survey the earth below, you can see the beach two hundred feet beneath you. The land below you glides slowly by and your mind settles on the hang glider that supports you. You grip the trapeze. A slight shift of your weight backwards and you soar higher.

You begin to look for a safe landing place below. You start to lean forward on the **control bar** as the glider eases downward. The sand on the beach gets closer and closer. Your feet almost touch the ground. All at once, the sand is beneath your feet and you run to a stop. You have landed safely. Wow!

To glide through the air high above the earth on a hang glider offers a special joy. You soar like a bird. Hang gliding, also known as "sky sailing" is a popular sport because it is thrilling to do and fun to watch.

Hang gliders do not have any kind of motor or engine. In most other ways they fly like any other aircraft. Hang gliders can stay up in the air for hours. Some expert gliders enjoy cross-country and mountain flying.

Hang gliders come in many forms, designs, and colors. Some are shaped like moths. Others are shaped like airplane wings.

Beginners often rent gliders for training until they become experts. They can then either buy or build one. Some hang gliders are built to support two flyers. This type may be used for training beginners.

Hang gliding is an adventure that can be enjoyed by anyone interested in an action sport that let's you glide, soar and sail like a bird.

Beginners often hang glide over beaches or low hills.

The hang glider has come a long way from the early designs of canvas and wood.

A SHORT HISTORY

People have always wanted to fly like birds. The problem is that we are much heavier than a bird. It takes more power than we can produce to take off by flapping wings. Over the years many ways have been tried to fly like the birds.

Hang gliding as we know it was invented in 1891 by Otto Lilienthal in Germany. As children, Otto and his brother Gustave, built many model gliders. As they grew up, they studied the way birds fly. One important discovery they made was how birds use their wings and change position as they soar through the air. In 1889, Otto published a book, <u>Bird Flight as the Basis of Aviation</u>.

In 1891 Otto built his first glider. The wing was 23 feet across. It was made of willow strips covered with waxed cotton cloth. He controlled the flight simply by shifting his body to change the *center of gravity.* The glider weighed about 40 pounds. This meant that it was light enough to launch from the top of a hill. Otto would run down the slope of the hill and the wind would pick him up.

The Lilienthal glider looked something like a huge pair of butterfly wings. He soared at about 35 miles per hour, to a height of about 100 feet.

Huge crowds watched Lilienthal and his hang glider. He made more than 2,000 short glides in his fixed-wing craft. He built many versions of his glider and always put them through a series of tests before flying in them. Unfortunately, in 1896 he was killed in a crash from a height of about 50 feet.

British aviation pioneer Percy Picher also made some valuable discoveries. As a child he was fascinated by the idea of flight. He built many model gliders. In 1893, at the age of 27, he built and flew his first glider. He called it the "Bat." The Bat had two wings that were laced together in the middle. They could fold back and forth like a fan. In his first experiment, he hovered about 12 feet above the ground for two to three minutes. In his most successful flight he was able to soar for about 60 feet at a height of 20 feet.

Then Picher decided to build a lightweight glider he called the "Gull." This one was too light as it did not work at all in a strong wind.

Next he built a glider he called the "Hawk." This one looked something like our modern airplane wings.

The Hawk was made of pine and was his best design. He was able to soar almost 300 yards in the Hawk, at a height of about 200 feet. Picher made many experiments with both fixed-wing gliders and powered machines. He, too, was killed in a crash, in 1899.

The Wright brothers first airplane was like a big glider with an engine. With all the excitement surrounding their flight in 1903, most people lost interest in hang gliding.

When World War II ended, many pilots who had been trained by the military still wanted to fly. But airplanes were expensive. What was needed was a simple, inexpensive flying device. People began to think of gliders again.

Dr. Francis Rogallo was an engineer who had spent World War II designing airplanes for the military. After 1945, he still worked for the goverment, but he and his wife Gertrude began to look at simple kite shapes. The Rogallo flexible wing design was used by the National Air and Space Agency, or NASA, in the 1960s. Reports of Rogallo's design were published in various magazines. People began to design frames to allow the Rogallo sailwing to carry a person.

John Dickenson, an Australian, was one of the first to add a control bar. This bar was part of the frame that hung below the sailwing. The flyer held onto the control bar and controlled the glider by shifting his weight. Two professional water skiers, Bill Bennett

Part of the fun of hang gliding is meeting other people interested in the same sport.

and Bill Moyes, began to use Dickenson's design in their act. They skied until the glider took off and then flew behind the boat.

When Bennett and Moyes came to the United States with their act, they met others who had had similar ideas. Gliders were made of plastic, bamboo, metal, silk, and nylon. Flyers took off from water skis, snow skis, and, sometimes, hills. In 1971, California glider fans held a big hang glider meet on Otto Lilienthal's birthday. One of the most successful designs at the meet looked like a big kite. It was the Rogallo wing on a frame that included a control bar and a seat. Modern hang gliding had been born.

*Taking off can be surprisingly difficult. The glider
wants to fly before you are ready to go.*

HOW TO GET STARTED

A hang glider resembles a flying wing and is made up of many parts. When it comes to function and handling, the sail is the most important part of the glider. It must be perfectly balanced. If it is out of alignment just a little bit, the craft will not fly properly.

Sails are usually made of Dacron, nylon, or some other lightweight but strong man-made fabric. The material is stretched across aluminum tubing called the control frame or A-frame. Sails can be anywhere from 13 feet to 28 feet across.

The sail is designed so it will have a good shape for flying. This is quite different from the way it looks in its relaxed state. As the frame holds the weight, it will flex and change the shape of the sail. The sail is attached to the frame with bolts or screws.

A cross tube keeps the leading edges of the wings at the correct angle. The wings are formed and stiffened by stretching them across thin bars called **battens**. The battens, or ribs of the glider, are built out of aluminum tubing, bamboo, fiberglass, or plywood. The hang glider is also kept in shape by **flying wires**.

The pilot hangs in a harness from the top of the control frame. The harness is connected to the frame

This sturdy glider is built for mountain gliding.

by webbing and cables. The cables are made from galvanized steel or stainless steel. This is for strength and durability. Some hang gliders are equipped with a sitting harness or swing seat. These seats make long flights more pleasant and enjoyable.

The pilot uses a control bar for steering. These are also called trapeze bars. A rounded, triangular control bar provides the best handling in the air. Padded bars make launching, carrying and landing a little more comfortable. Gliders that are controlled by the pilot shifting weight are used for flights which are low, slow and take place in smooth air. Higher altitudes, greater air speeds, or stronger wind conditions call for a glider with additional controls.

A lighter glider is useful for low-level gliding.

Most simple hang gliders weigh about 35 pounds. Some models have two wings. These are called biplanes. Biplanes also have rudders and more controls for steering. They can weigh up to 75 pounds.

The Rogallo-type hang glider is the most popular. The design is simple and lightweight. It is easy to transport and is not real expensive. It is also easy to build this type.

A hang glider depends on the wind and air currents. To launch or land the glider, the pilot uses his legs. In order to get the hang glider airborne, the pilot runs into the wind off a hill or cliff. Only a short run is necessary in order to take off and if the wind is blowing around 12 mph, the pilot can take off without running.

Once in the air, the gliders are controlled by the pilot shifting his weight. A hang glider must be the right size for the weight of the pilot. If it is too small, it will fly too fast and sink quickly. If it is too big, it is hard to control.

When learning to fly a hang glider, each trip is a new adventure. The gentle slope of a hill or big sand dune can be a good place for a brief ride. Some pilots who have been flying for many years enjoy flying longer distances. Besides the great feeling of flying, cross-country pilots can enjoy the scenery.

A hang glider, like the one in the long bag on the ground, is surprisingly small when it's folded for travel.

Practicing take-offs down a gentle hill in a simple Rogallo wing glider.

To fly a long distance, you need to find a good air current. These air currents are called thermals. Thermals are huge masses of rising warm air. Thermals are formed when the ground becomes warm. This warmth heats the air above it. Hot air rises and it will carry a hang glider. A good rising air current can be hard to find, so it is important that the pilot uses special instruments. The air speed indicator tells how fast or slow the hang glider is going, the variometer shows whether the glider is losing or gaining altitude and the altimeter gives the altitude.

How air currents are formed depends on the type of ground, the weather, and the time of day. Flat fields and low lying towns warm up quickly. Forests take longer to warm. Heavily wooded areas, though, retain their heat until late in the day. Cross-country flyers notice these kinds of signs when they look for thermals.

SAFETY TIPS

The first time a new glider is flown, the pilot should be very careful. Every glider has its own particular feel. A pilot must become familiar with all the individual features of a new glider.

Hang gliders do not need to get a license. They still must obey the rules of flight and air traffic laws. All users of air space over the United States must obey Federal Aviation Administration rules. These rules apply whether you fly an airplane or a kite.

Hang glider pilots need to obey the rules concerning right-of-way in the sky. An aircraft in distress always has the right-of-way. Hot air balloons are next in line for the right-of-way. They are followed by tow planes and gliders. If there is some doubt as to who has the right-of-way, always yield. Courtesy is never wrong.

Many hang gliding clubs specialize in providing safety education and guidance. Lightweight, low-speed hang gliding is rarely a danger to persons and property on the ground. The most common injuries to pilots are broken arms during bad landings.

Here are some safety guidelines. If you follow these suggestions, serious injuries can be avoided.

The fully-equipped hang glider wears safety harness, helmet, and parachute.

When flying at this height, a parachute is required in case of accidents

Pilots of hang gliders should wear lightweight, protective clothing and gloves. A helmet is strongly recommended.

Do not fly a glider during a storm, in bad weather, or if gusty or very high wind conditions exist.

Do not fly a hang glider in an airport traffic area, or within five miles of any airport unless you have obtained permission.

Do not fly a hang glider within any prohibited or restricted area without permission.

Do not fly a hang glider within 100 feet of buildings, populated places, or crowds.

Avoid sailing into clouds, large flocks of birds, telephone poles and wires.

Trees are another hazard to watch for.

MOUNTAIN FLYING

Some of the most exciting flights can be enjoyed in the high mountains. This is not like flying from small hills. Air currents operate differently in the mountains. It can be much more difficult to identify the signs of lifting air.

Because mountain air is thinner, a faster take off speed must be reached. A specially built ramp may be required for launching. The unusual wind patterns can make launching the hang glider a problem. Only the most experienced pilots should attempt high mountain flying.

Mountain flying requires a big, strong,hang glider. It must be larger than the type used for low, slow gliding from gentle slopes or sand dunes at beaches. Some special equipment is also useful for high mountain flying. For flying over snow covered peaks, a **cocoon** harness is needed. It resembles a sleeping bag, and will keep the pilot warm. Because of its streamlined shape, it offers little air resistance and will increase speed.

When they go very high in the mountains, pilots take air tanks with them as well as warm clothing.

From the earliest days of the sport, pilots have always wanted to see who could fly farther, faster, and better.

COMPETITIONS AND RECORDS

Hang gliding is an international sport. Competitions often draw pilots from around the world. These sporting events give them a chance to meet other people who share their love of gliding. They also learn new techniques and exchange ideas about improving their skills.

In the summertime, a ski resort makes for a good place to hold competitions. The slopes provide excellent launch points and good places for spectators to watch. Ski hills also have tows, which make getting to the top easier. The Hawaiian islands also offer strong, soaring winds. These are suitable for many kinds of competition.

In southern California, competitions are held at the Torrey Pines Gliderport. The launch site is located atop a towering, 360 foot sandstone bluff overlooking Black's Beach. This is an excellent place for expert flyers. For specific information about competitions, contact the Gliderport at La Jolla Village Farms Rd., La Jolla, CA (619)457-9093.

There are numerous types of competitions for hang gliders. Some events measure the skill and accuracy of a pilot. In a **pylon task** contest, pilots must fly around special markers, forming a pattern. The one that gets closest to the markers and follows the pattern wins. Because of difficult terrain, sometimes real pylons cannot be used as markers and judges cannot be positioned at every point. The pilots must photograph the turning points as evidence of having rounded them.

There are other kinds of events, too. Some contests measure the greatest straight line distance flown from the launch. In 1983, an outstanding British pilot, John Pendry, set the official world distance record. Flying an Airwave Magic 3 from California to Nevada, he flew 186.8 miles. At the same time, another British pilot, Judy Leden, set the distance record for women of 145.3 miles.

The record for the greatest gain of height was set in California in 1985. A U.S. pilot, Larry Tudor, reached a height of 14,150 feet from his take-off spot.

There will always be new records to break for the longest flight and the highest flight. As long as the skies are clear and the wind is right, hang gliders will continue to make new records.

Pilots have to watch carefully for the markers on the course.

A group gathers around a parasailor on the beach.

PARASAILING

Parasailing is like hang gliding in many ways. You fly through the air, but instead of piloting a glider, you hang from a parachute. Parasailing takes places over water and requires the use of a motorboat.

The parasail is somewhat like a regular parachute. It is made of the same material, nylon.

Water skiers got the idea of using parachutes. They inflated a small parachute while they were being towed by a motorboat. It lifted them into the air. A swing seat was attached and parasailing was born.

Parasailing is more of a recreational activity than a sport. Parasailors do not have races and competitions. It is something you do just for fun. Many people parasail for the first time while on vacation. The coasts of California, Mexico, and the Hawaiian islands offer parasailing all year round. The warm climate and miles of shoreline are perfect for parasailing.

Parasailing is an activity that is open to everyone. No steering ability or special skills are required. Even people with a disability, such as blindness, can enjoy parasailing.

Parasailors begin as passengers on a boat. Besides a life jacket, no unusual clothing or extra equipment is

![parasailor carrying parachute]

Some parasail businesses require all parasailors to wear helmets.

needed. Most of the same safety guidelines for hang gliding apply to parasailing. Although parasailing takes place over water, you do not have to get wet. Parasailors go directly from the boat into the air, and then back into the boat.

A 26 foot parachute is the average size for most parasailors. This size chute needs to carry a minimum of ninety pounds to remain open and balanced. A parasailor can rise up to 300 feet into the air.

Morning is the best time of day to go parasailing. The water is usually calm then, so the boat ride is smooth to give an even lift off of the parasail.

A parasail ride can last from a few minutes to an hour. If the wind dies down, the boat can go a little faster. This will create enough wind to keep the parachute aloft.

In the early days of parasailing, a platform on the beach was used for take offs and landings. Sometimes just a stretch of beach was used. The parachute was attached to a motorboat by a strong

Towing the parasailor aloft from the beach was a tricky task.

cable. The harness attached to the parachute allowed the parasailor to stand upright. The motorboat would pull away from the beach. The parasailor would run forward until the wind caught the chute. Sometimes the parasailor got wet before getting up.

Landings were not always easy. The boat would head in towards the beach and start going slower. As the wind died down, the parasailor would get closer to the beach. As the boat pulled to a stop, the parasailor would drop to the sand. Sometimes the parasailor would drop in the water, instead of the beach. Injuries like a broken arm or ankle could happen during a bad landing.

One of the early parasailors, Guy Ciletti, decided there must be a better way to launch and land a parasail. He noticed that most injuries seemed to occur during bad landings on the beach. He thought it might be better to take off and land on the boat.

First he designed a hydraulic winch to fit on his 27 foot speed boat. This winch would control the cable attached to the parachute. The next step was to avoid take off accidents that happened from running on the beach. He did this by attaching a swing seat to the parachute. Now passengers in his boat could get into the sitting harness and take off from there.

Parasails don't offer the pilot as much control as hang gliders do.

The hydraulic winch let out the cable as the parasailor rose into the air. Take off could not be easier. When it was time to land, the boat would slow down. Then the winch would pull in the cable until the parasailor was back in the boat.

FOR MORE INFORMATION

Hang gliding lessons are available all along the coastlines of the United States. For more information contact Kitty Hawk Kites, Reservation Road/ Route 1, Monterey, CA (408)384-2622; Hang Gliding Center, 4206 Sorrento Valley Center, Del Mar, CA (619)450-9008; Chandelle Hang Gliding Center, 488 Manor Plaza, Pacifica, CA (415)359-6800.

Hang gliding and parasailing are fun, thrilling sports the entire family can enjoy. You can sail over waves lapping at the shore or tree tops whistling in the wind. Whether you fly in the sky or watch from below, it is an experience you will long remember.

Some of the most experienced hang glider pilots do tricks and loops—not recommended for beginners!

GLOSSARY

Angle of attack: the angle of the hang glider wing as it meets the air flow.

Battens: rods of fiberglass or a similar material. They are placed in the wing to give it shape and hold it firm.

Cocoon: a streamlined covering the pilot gets into. It is used for speed and to keep warm at high altitudes.

Control bar: the bar at the bottom of the triangular control frame suspended from the wings. To change direction, the pilot holds the control bar and shifts his weight.

Flying wires: wires that connect the control frame and other parts of the glider. The wires keep the correct shape of the glider and strengthen its structure.

Launch ramp: a sloping take off area built to help take off from difficult places.

Microlight: a type of hang glider powered by a small engine.

Pylon task: a contest in which the pilots have to fly a course marked with pylons.

Ridge: a long, even hill ideal for hang gliding because of the regular currents of air flowing up and over its top surface.

Rogallo wing: a triangular shaped hang glider. It is named after Dr. Francis Rogallo whose work led to the modern hang glider.

Stall: the loss of smooth airflow over the wings. It results in a sudden loss of lift.

Thermal: a rising current of warm air. Glider pilots use thermals to gain height.

INDEX